Dissecting the
ETHICAL HACKER

A guide for the Wine 'n Cheese Crowd
(a.k.a. Suits & Technology Leaders)

Michael Willburn
Illustrated by the Author

www.HaxorusEthicus.com

ISBN-10: 1483963160
ISBN-13: 978-1483963167

To my lovely wife and beautiful kids

CONTENTS

PREFACE

Lean comfortably back in your plush leather chair, steal a sip of crisp and fruity Sauvignon Blanc, nibble thoughtfully on a fresh multi-grain cracker spread with aged Gorgonzola, and allow me to dissect for you the strange but wonderful breed of the Ethical Hacker. What do they look like? How do you spot 'em in a crowded data center? How might you catch and tame one of these odd beasts? Sip your Sauvignon, read on, and all will be revealed.

Organizations like SANs, Black Hat, Offensive Security, DefCon and others are churning out highly skilled Ethical Hackers by the hundreds. Each one of these little fellas and fellettes is taking their newly found hacking skills back to your organization where they gather together like hungry wolves; red-eyes glowing wildly, they chase your innocent systems around your data center like frightened little rabbits.

Too frequently this wild pack of Ethical Hackers adds little real value to the never ending process of securing your organization. Now, this is not because they lack the skills; quite the contrary, they have plenty of very impressive technical skills and an entire new language to boot. No, they are not adding value simply because the poor sod (i.e. you) that has to manage these beasts and make business decisions based on their work is not quite sure how to use them effectively. This new breed of Techie needs leadership, needs guidance, needs perspective and sometimes they even need to be taken behind the woodshed for a good old-fashioned talking-to.

While the stores are overflowing with books that teach folks how to become Ethical Hackers, there are hardly any resources available to teach corporate leaders how to effectively utilize this rapidly increasing breed. A quick search of on-line bookstores will produce few, if any, results for building and leading teams of Ethical Hackers. Most authors focus on high-level risk management topics or in-the-weeds 'how to' hacking guides.

The result? Too many organizations underuse their Ethical Hackers, simply validating compliance rather than adding real value to the security of their organizations. Others spend millions of dollars trying to chase each and every "vulnerability" their staff comes across – ignorant of the true significance of these risks and led by the nose

3

as a result of this ignorance.

Now your worries are over. As you sip your wine and nibble on your crackers you will learn all about the individual breeds of Ethical Hackers, their likes and dislikes, and how they communicate with each other. Best of all, you will learn what they are doing to your systems and how to use their skills to improve the security of your organization.

Please take a moment to refill your wine glass. Might I suggest a California Zinfandel as it pairs well with what you are about to read, that is, material which is delicately balanced, has an unobtrusive bouquet, is not too complex, and has an ever so slight hint of dry humor.

EVOLUTION OF THE SPECIES

A New Evolutionary Branch is Growing in the Tech-
Animal Kingdom, the *Haxorus ethicus*,
The Ethical Hacker

Ethical Hackers are similar to others in the technology world, in that they come in many sizes, shapes and colors. Contrary to popular belief, they are not a one-size fits all breed. In fact, through years of careful, controlled studies, I have identified no less than twelve distinct breeds – each with its own unique personality, approach to conducting security assessments, and leadership or "handling" needs.

Some of these breeds should be chased down, captured and tamed while others need to be avoided at all costs. To begin to understand the Ethical Hacker animal, you must first understand these primary breeds, and to do so, you will need to tune into your inner-anthropologist.

Let's begin at...well...the beginning. It is tempting for some of us refined individuals in the Wine'n Cheese Crowd to want to classify the Ethical Hacker as knuckle-walkers, under the subfamily of hominid. While some do display the characteristics of knuckle-walkers, they are more accurately classified under a new species of *Homo sapiens* called *Haxorus ethicus or H. ethicus* for short. This new species can be traced down the evolutionary line of *Homo sapiens* to a common ancestor, the *Homo technus*.

Nowadays, there are thousands of offshoots of *Homo technus* working in information technology shops and running billion dollar technology corporations...but theirs is a story for another time.

A few decades ago *Homo technus'* evolutionary path split when a few of the coastal species began to develop a new curiosity towards computers that went beyond the wonders of switching out punch cards and vacuum tubes. In the early 1980's an important DNA mutation occurred when a few curious *Homo technus* found they could make free phone calls with common cereal box toys. But chatting on the phone into the wee morning hours about Dungeons and Dragons strategies or warning fellow Leisure Suit Larry gamers that they needed to remember to stop by the convenience store before chatting with that prostitute, quickly got old.

Perhaps it started with a mis-typed phone number (evolution is still a bit of a mystery), but they soon found they could use their free phone service to have more interesting

A new species has emerged from the dark depths of their mom's basement, the *Haxorus ethicus* – Ethical Hacker.

conversations with corporate and military systems using a dial-up modem and personal computer. Around this same time the movie War Games hit the theaters, creating ripples and waves among the technically curious and forever splitting the evolutionary path of *Homo technus*. A new species had emerged from the dark, dank bowels of their mother's basement.

Like other technical species, *Haxorus ethicus* has a highly-developed brain capable of abstract reasoning, language, and problem solving; but they have evolved a few unique characteristics that separate them from the others. Chief among these new characteristics is their intense curiosity not just about how things work but more specifically, how they could make things work in ways which they were not intended to by their creators.

Using Capt'n Crunch toys to make pretty whistling noises – while fun – was not as fun as figuring out that the toy could emit a tone at a frequency of 2600 hertz[1]. Interestingly, this was the same frequency that AT&T used to put a phone line into operator mode – ultimately allowing them to make free calls around the world. With a bit of curious playing around these fellas and fellettes had figured out how to make a simple pay phone wipe its brow and say, "Whew! I never knew I had it in me."

Over the years *Haxorus ethicus* has refined its abilities to break into computer systems quicker than you can pop the cork on that bottle of red. While *Homo technus* is busy writing code and building systems to solve complex business problems, *Haxorus ethicus* is using these systems like an Aikido master; manipulating them and redirecting their energy in ways the developers were not expecting. Like determined prisoners serving a life

---

[1] As a side note, in later years this frequency was used as the name of a popular hacker's magazine, *2600: The Hacker Quarterly*.

sentence, they work patiently in their basements, cubicles and offices – chiseling their way into and out of your systems.

Another key distinction to be aware of between *Homo technus* and *Haxorus ethicus* is their differing approaches to tools. While most technical species have evolved their tool making skills to help them create technical solutions to complex business problems, *Haxorus ethicus* spends all its time creating highly sophisticated tools to help it break these very same creations.

It has refined its tool-making skills, creating a body of specialized tools to, for example, snoop network traffic. It snoops network traffic not for the purpose of troubleshooting network performance or connectivity issues as the *Homo technus* might but rather to eavesdrop on conversations, steal sensitive information, or play monkey-in-the-middle games – pun intended.

The tools it has created fuzz protocols, identify hidden components of systems, manipulate network packets, strip encryption, and even allow it to manage relational databases from a single parameter on a web application. They are a breed of their own and, like Darwin, we can dissect them to better understand what makes 'em tick.

Please take a moment to top off your glass of wine and grab some more crackers before you read on.

DISSECTING
THE VARIOUS BREEDS

Exploring the Unique Types of *Haxorus ethicus*,
The Ethical Hacker

As mentioned, there are no less than a dozen distinct breeds of *Haxorus ethicus* or the Ethical Hacker. For your amusement and convenience I have cataloged them into short profiles. While these profiles are obviously a bit tongue-in-cheek (just a bit) they actually represent the various approaches Ethical Hackers take when performing their work (we'll look at their work a little later). If you can peel back some of the layers of my twisted sense of humor, and I admit this is not often easy, then you will learn how to identify the various approaches, some of the pros and cons of each approach, and some sage management advice.

Learn about the various types of Ethical Hackers and the approaches they use to assess the security of your system.

The following profiles include a brief description of the breed, some identification and handling tips, and to assist with identification, their root dance style. For those that are confused by the root dance, this is the dance your Ethical Hacker will do when he or she breaks into your company's system and gains privileged (God-like) access. Gaining access to a command prompt running with root privileges will immediately precede the dance.

But let us stop beating around the bush and jump into dissecting the primary breeds of *Haxorus ethicus*.

Dissecting the Various Breeds

"Destroius Maximus"

Ramb-acker

Summary

As the name suggests, this breed of Ethical Hacker will fire everything in their arsenal at company systems. Whatever security tool you can think of, they not only own it but can break it down and put it back together in less than a minute – blindfolded. All of the security tools they possess have pet names, like "Susie" or "George." On the plus side, they will do a good job of finding vulnerabilities on systems. On the bad side, they will do a good job of finding vulnerabilities on systems, including the gazillion ways to DoS everything – from the printers to the mainframes.

In addition to their rather frightening knowledge of technology and obsession with security tools, they will also possess the ability to go hand-to-hand with systems using their manual hacker skills. With their command line Kung Fu they will silently sneak up behind an innocently grazing server and stick a K-bar through its motherboard. Indeed, they have been known to snap a system peripheral in twain with the speed and power of Chuck Norris.

Identification

Thankfully they are not too difficult to identify. There are obvious characteristics, such as flash drives loaded with security tools chained together on a belt draped around a naked and scarred shoulder. These flash drives feed a belt-fed USB hub, which they attach to a juiced up laptop that can fire three gazillion packets per second at your systems. When they enter the data center a wave of silence will crash over the place and all the little blinky lights on the servers will freeze. Like young gazelles hiding in the grass as the hungry lion stalks nearby, your servers will shiver uncontrollably and spontaneously pop up a terminal window running as root when *Destroius Maximus* struts by. In the board room, they will gaze with wild eyes at your system architecture diagram as you brief them about the "targets" and "scope." With drool dripping onto your Viso diagrams, they will ask rapid "to-the-point" questions, cutting short your response with another question.

Handling Tips

Handle with care, or your data center may become a smoking hole in the ground when they are done with their security assessment. However, when deployed properly, they will do quality work and be especially comprehensive with their assessment. Of course, watch that they are not too comprehensive attacking your business partners, employees, next door neighbors, etc. Like most Ethical Hackers, they'll need a well defined scope and some pretty clear rules of engagement.

Root Dance

Destroius Maximus reeks of confidence, they expect root

and are rarely disappointed. Like an aged rock star tired of the groupies grabbing at him, they have seen those terminal windows running as root many times before. Indeed, they have sometimes seen two, three or more terminal windows at the same time on a single system and all running as root. When they gain root they may display a quick Mick Jagger hand move and head tilt, or some Steven Tyler inspired footwork but often they will simply keep firing away at the system.

"Me-us Abouticus"

Narcissistic Hacker

Summary

For this breed, security assessments are not about the security of their customers' systems as much as they are about having a platform to display their own fabulous hacking skills. The *Me-us Abouticus* is a dangerous breed of Ethical Hacker and you should proceed with caution if you spot one poking around your data center. This little guy will cost organizations time, money and stress; forcing system administrators, developers and the like to chase every "critical" vulnerability without consideration of significance or impact to the organization.

Identification

This little fella – and they come in fellettes too - will have you believing they are immortals sent to you from Mount Olympus. They will make liberal use of popular buzzwords and use complex technical phrases that may or may not make technical sense. Technical prowess cannot be utilized as an aid to identification because one may be extremely knowledgeable, technically speaking, while another may be an incompetent buffoon who has taken a course on Ethical Hacking, mastered the buzzwords and simple tools, and is now a leet h@xor.

In general, they will make themselves known to you by standing atop the desk or table from which they are working and vociferously pat themselves on the back every time they discover a vulnerability in your systems.

Dissecting the Ethical Hacker
A guide for the Wine'n Cheese Crowd

In conversations about the security assessment underway on your systems, they will avoid explaining the real significance of the vulnerabilities they discovered but rather focus on the mere fact that *they* found them and you are screwed. In fact, if you question them about significance and risk, they will be offended that you are selfishly attempting to shift the focus from their achievements to the security of your silly little system.

Handling Tips

Handle with extreme care if you realize that you have one on your team. Make sure you peer-review their findings using knowledgeable team members, and do not allow them to work alone. Often they will stop the security assessment once they find a vulnerability, so you will want to ensure they complete the security assessment of the system even after they find that little nugget they are parading around. Someone will need to stop their parade and put them back to work because the "game" is not "over." Also, thoroughly review any reports to ensure they balance the "cool factor" with the "analysis of why you should care and what you should do."

Root Dance

Root dance style will resemble Hip Hop dancing such as Breaking, Electric Boogaloo, the Robot, and such. Some *Me-us Abouticus* will incorporate a short high pitched cry into their routine along with moon-walking and grabbing of the nether region.

"Theoreticus Maximus"

Academic Hacker

Summary

This breed of Ethical Hacker dwells primarily in the world of theory rather than practicality. *Theoreticus Maximus* usually has multiple doctoral degrees in a variety of technical areas and has read every book on cyber security, possibly even written a few themselves. They will be well-versed in the theoretical aspects of threats, threat vectors, and known vulnerabilities.

The pure blooded will have chalkboards near their desk covered in mathematical proofs for theoretical vulnerabilities; but like the existence of dark matter, these proofs will be the mere speculation of large-brained individuals with crazy gray hair. *Theoreticus Maximus* will be very articulate and logical when discussing both the methods one should follow for conducting security assessments and how those results should be presented. But despite their vast knowledge, and degree-painted walls, they will likely have never actually performed the work of an Ethical Hacker on anything other than a chalkboard.

Identification

If the wall of fancy framed degrees or chalkboard does not give them away, then you can oust one by asking a simple question to a small gathering of Ethical Hackers. It does not matter what the question is, just make it simple. The *Theoreticus Maximus* will simultaneously raise her hand as she springs to her feet. Once called upon, she will tip her head and look straight at you over the top of her spectacles and respond in a manner that makes you and all those gathered around feel as if you have been transported back to elementary school. Her answer may take hours, days, or even weeks, and will likely include a PowerPoint presentation with graphic representations of the information presented. She may offer to research certain aspects for you in more depth and will of course, present you with her bibliography so that you may scrutinize her sources of information.

If you have never seen one before and wish to catch a reliable glimpse, then simply go down to your local Big-4 consulting agency, and there you will find herds of them grazing among the "hot desks," plucked straight from the classroom and made into "road warriors."

Handling Tips

If used appropriately, they can be a great resource, especially when it comes to writing plans and reports. They will make the less articulate on your team shine, backing up all their findings with detailed explanations of *"the what," "the how,"* and *"the now what the heck do I do?"* But remember, *Theoreticus Maximus* will be far more comfortable talking about what needs to be done and how to do it but not in the least bit comfortable actually doing the work of an Ethical Hacker in the real world. They can write you a thousand page thesis about what to do and how to do it but they just cannot bring themselves to actually pull the trigger and do the work themselves.

Nevertheless, if you recognize this fact, and have other 'doers' on your team, then they are worth nurturing and keeping around. But take care, as no team can sustain too many *Theoreticae Maximi* at one time. There will be great conversations, plenty of intellectual stimuli, but no work will actually get done.

Root Dance

Most have only seen a terminal window with root level access in the lab environment or read about it in books. Nevertheless, they have developed a rather amusing and unique root dance among Ethical Hackers. The dance is comparable to watching an English teacher who is chaperoning the high school prom. Wearing a black leather jacket and tight jeans, they stand in the shadows off the dance floor spastically busting moves every few seconds and then quickly regaining their composure.

"Limitus Oculus"
Myopic Hacker

Summary

When working their Ethical Hacking magic on a system, *Limitus Oculus* will focus solely on locating a single type of vulnerability or will exhaustively search a single component of a system for a potential vulnerability – all the while ignoring the majority of the system.

For example, pretend for a moment your organization has spent millions building a massive server farm, placing in the stables of the data center mail servers, multiple web application servers, identity management systems, database servers, a complex network management infrastructure with layers of separation, and all using multiple flavors of operating systems; Solaris, Linux, Windows, etc. *Limitus Oculus* will spend five days, of a five day vulnerability assessment of this infrastructure, fuzzing a single parameter on *one* of the web applications in your server farm or spend their entire time searching for missing patches on only the Windows servers. They are hyper-focused (not necessarily in a good way), as they look at systems with tunnel vision, missing even the most obvious vulnerability that exists outside of their limited scope.

Identification

Easy to spot. Simply ask, "What are you up to?" Make note of the response and ask again in an hour, two hours, a day, etc. The answers will all be the same.

In a gaggle of Ethical Hackers, they will be the ones desperate to find zero days at any cost. They will launch themselves so far into a component of a system that the actual weeds of the system will be above them. Another way to positively identify one is to ask the suspected *Limitus Oculus* what their favorite security assessment tool is. If they say a fuzzer, decompiler or hex editor then it is a safe bet you are dealing with *Limitus Oculus*.

Handling Tips

You will not get a comprehensive security assessment of the system out of these little fellas and fellettes without a cattle prod. Try to identify why they are so hyper-focused. For example, is it that they focus on a single technology or component because they are not comfortable with anything else? Or is it simply that they are desperate to make a name for themselves by finding that zero-day?

Handling techniques may need to be modified once their motivation is understood. Nevertheless, once identified, make sure they are given timelines for tasks and proper direction and oversight. You will find yourself having to be creative at times, i.e. "I'll let you fuzz that binary after you've finished XY and Z." Now, if all you want is to assess a specific component, then toss it to one of these guys and they will tear at it like a terrier with a bone. Just watch your hand when you try to get it back from them –

they might bite if they aren't done gnawing on it.

Root Dance

Root dance style is high-energy experimental, similar to Raving, and will almost always include a laser light show as accompaniment. Take care if you are nearby when they discover root as they may leap off a desk and expect the crowd to catch them.

" *Canius Antiquus* "

Old Dog Hacker

Summary

Most large institutions have a few *Canius Antiqui* roaming the firths and fjords of their data centers. These individuals are the only ones that know how to make the lights on that Doctor Who'esque box in the back of the data center light up like the dash board of the TARDIS. They have been around for eons and remember the days before "micro computing machines" when life was simple and all one had to do was swap out punch cards and change a vacuum tube every once in a blue moon – a time when the speed of your computer's processor could be increased by simply adding another row of beads to your abacus.

Do not mistake them with *H. ethicus " Experiencus"*, who has been around since the dawn of computing but has also managed to keep his skills current. *Canius Antiquus* was certainly around when computers were powered by water mills and mules but they unfortunately have not kept up to date with the present world of computing. *Canius Antiquus* is not comfortable unless the computing machine is the size of a room and will actively resist any attempts to force them to understand even the simplest modern concepts. They do not like to...ahem...learn new tricks.

Identification

They are slow moving and easy to spot. In fact, simply

approach a herd of grazing Ethical Hackers in the company kitchen and then toss in a verbal bomb like, "They are handing out free iPhones in front of the building!" Be careful not to get trampled by the herd as they scramble for the door but do watch the kitchen area as they move off down the hall towards the elevators. After the dust settles, poke your head back into the company kitchen and there you will find *Canius Antiquus* loitering around the refrigerator with a jar of Ovaltine in his hands.

Other ways to spot them are to simply engage your suspected *Canius Antiquus* in a conversation about the Internet and their favorite websites. Their eyes will likely glaze over and they may actually nod off while you speak. If they do respond, they will usually use terms like "Interneting", "Windowing", and "World Wide Webbing".

Handling Tips

They will not be impressed with your new-fangled technologies. They are convinced that this whole personal computing thing is a fad and society will soon return to the good old days of computers the size of a five-ton truck. Therefore, attempting to educate them on new technologies is like a broken pencil – pointless. They are riding Father Time like a beaten mule, just waiting for him to ride them off into the sunset of retirement. Now, if you have one of those Doctor Who'esque machines running in your data center, then you will have to indulge this individual until you can replace the machine with an iPod. But if you decommissioned your last TARDIS, then you might want to smack the mule on the butt and move *Canius Antiquus* along or at least some place where his skills will be more useful.

Therefore, when it comes to assessing the quality of their work, and if it has to do with modern computing, you must question them thoroughly. If they refer to that Dalek-looking machine roaming your data center and vaporizing other servers in its path then you are in a tough spot. Who really knows what they are even talking about? After all, these are machines that take a week to boot up and require a reboot for even the simplest configuration changes such as updating the system time for daylight savings.

Root Dance

Root level access has a whole different meaning for them. They are used to seeing terminal windows with privileged access and indeed do not really understand concepts like "least privilege" or "separation of duty." So no root dance per se, but they have been seen to move their hands effortlessly across their keyboard like a Jazz pianist – cigarette hanging out of their mouth and a glass of whiskey resting close by.

"Metrosexualus"

GQ Hacker

Summary

The runway models of the ethical hacking community, they are dead sexy and can break into your systems quicker than you can complement their Italian leather shoes. These folks not only hack your systems but they look damn good while doing so. They are clean, organized, and have a strange obsession with pointy tipped shoes, French perfume and choker necklaces.

Metrosexualus will have an outfit for each hacking occasion, and their attire will almost always be color-coordinated with the system currently under assessment. The good news is that most will want the results of their security testing to look and smell as sexy as they do. They are distant cousins of the *Me-us Abouticus,* but this breed developed a sense of professionalism and perspective that the former never quite achieved.

Identification

The challenge is to be able to distinguish *Metrosexualus* from *Me-us Abouticus.* The main difference is self-confidence. *Metrosexualus* will not be obsessed with proving themselves, like *Me-us Abouticus* always is, as they have a great deal of self-confidence. In any case, the pleasure of gazing upon their shining personage while they work should be enough for anyone.

They do not need to prove anything to anybody – they know they are good. In fact, they are so good that they have a knack for convincing giddy system administrators to massage their necks while they hack away at a server console during late night assessments. Another surefire technique for identification of the female of the breed is to ask where she bought her shoes. If she responds, "Christian Louboutin spent two weeks studying my feet, taking my feet to dinner, spending quality time with my feet, creating moldings of them and then jetted back to his Parisian studio where he spent a year designing custom shoes for every one of my hacking occasions," well, it is a safe bet you are dealing with a female *Metrosexualus*.

Handling Tips

Keep'em focused, especially when travelling to customer sites as they will want to stop at every shoe store along the way. The males may get distracted easily by the women in the office but this may come in handy when social engineering information out of a giddy system administrator. The good news is they will take criticism better than *Me-us Abouticus* as they have a sincere desire to be the best and the self-confidence to take constructive criticism. Also, they may be overly elaborate in reports, but they are usually professional, and their findings will always be verified — they do not like embarrassment as it puts a chink in the Sir Lancelot image they have of themselves. One downside is that their perfume can sometimes make you feel as though you have taken a shot of pepper spray directly in the face. Therefore, you may find it difficult to remain conscious while working with them in confined spaces.

Root Dance

The root dance of Metrosexualus is something special — at least in their minds. Like a runway model who knows she looks stunning, when they gain root, they will start to strut through the aisles of the data center while pouting their lips and violently swinging their hips to and fro. They will exhibit their root level access like a mink coat draped seductively over their shoulder, tossing a smile and a wink to each team member as they pass by.

"Egomaniacus Technum"

Elitist Hacker

Summary

A familiar breed, we see these little guys on many different branches of the tech-animal tree. They are a close cousin of the Narcissistic Hacker but each possesses its own unique characteristics. *Egomaniacus Technum* is usually a master of a single technology, such as a programming language, operating system or application, and will dismiss all other technologies and those individuals that use them as ignoramuses. In the security world they tend to gravitate towards a single operating system(often but not always UNIX), and they rarely use any security assessment tool they did not personally develop. If they do use other security tools, they are usually open source tools that they modified to "get them working properly."

In general, you will be made to feel small in their company as they know more than you or anybody you know or will ever know in your lifetime.

Identification

There is often no question that you are, in fact, dealing with an *Egomaniacus Technum* because only moments after letting anything even slightly technical leave your lips, they will instantly shrink you down to the size of a door mouse, and you will regret having spoken at all. They will likely not hear a word you have to say and will always find fault with the designers, developers and

administrators of the system they are assessing –
frequently alluding to these individuals as clueless
neophytes.

There are a few techniques you can use to confirm the
identity of a suspected *Egomaniacus Technum*. For
example, if you suspect that the individual is of the
operating system oriented breed, then simply say (in
general terms), that Microsoft has done wonders for the
world of security. If they are of the Microsoft breed then
they will smirk and launch into a lecture that will
culminate in a statement or insinuation about how little
you knew about Microsoft's contributions to the world
of security. If you mention Internet Explorer 6 or say you
find Ubuntu easier to secure than Windows 7 (whether
you believe this or not) they will instantly chastise you
and make you feel like a UNIX-loving hippie beatnik with
no understanding of what Bill did for the world of
computing.

Interestingly, a once endangered subspecies from this
branch – the *Macintus Loveruscus* – has made an
amazing comeback in the past few years and, in fact, is
now commonly spotted roaming with packs of Ethical
Hackers.

Handling Tips

Handle these folks with care as their egos are often
fragile, and if their opinions or judgment is questioned,

they may attack. But do not show them fear or back down too easily or you will find it difficult controlling them. Often, it is best to question their results alone rather than in front of the team so they do not feel threatened. Let them win when it doesn't matter. Take care in understanding the advice they provide as they may make you or your customer feel like an idiot for not immediately comprehending their assessment of the system.

Root Dance

When *Egomaniacus Technum* achieves root the lights will dim in the data center and a disco ball will descend from the ceiling. He will cry out, "Yooowza, baby. Man I dig this gig!" as he throws back his chair, grabs a rack of servers and spins out into the center of the data center floor. Thrusting his hips into your system and slowly wrapping one arm around the back of the rack, he will swing and sway like the disco kings of old.

"Novellus"

Neophyte Hacker

Summary

Novellus, as one might guess from the name, is the fella that is new to the world of ethical hacking. Often they are former developers, systems administrators, network engineers, and such, who are in the early stages of the Ethical Hacker metamorphosis. Therefore, they are typically very technical but they are just not used to being ethically evil, that is, they have yet to learn how to use their technical skills in the realm of the Ethical Hacker. In their hearts and minds they still think like builders rather than breakers of technology.

Identification

These guys and gals are fairly easy to identify because they are the ones that prefer to discuss technology, whichever technology it is they know, rather than security. They are still transitioning from the world of fixing things to the world of breaking things, so they tend to be a bit gentle and forgiving when they perform the work of an Ethical Hacker.

For example, when conducting a web application assessment, *Novellus* will use the application *exactly* as it was intended to be used. If there is a form requesting a name and address then that is precisely what they will input into the fields on the form. This is in contrast to other Ethical Hackers who will input everything *but* a name and address - to include every special character, number and letter with every possible encoded variation. When *Novellus* notices one of their teammates misusing an application, they will typically cry out, "Hey, you shouldn't do that! That's not how the application works." The response to such an outburst is, "yes, I know. That is the *hacking* part of ethical hacking."

Handling Tips

If they can be turned to the dark side, that is to say, the ethical dark side, then they will prove to be a powerful ally. Turning them is easier said than done. Coming from the world of information technology where they were trained to build and fix things, they will find it difficult to think outside the box.

Novellus is best when paired up with the more mature and experienced on your team – though you will find many will prove useful simply because of their in-depth knowledge of a specific technology. When they are paired with a seasoned Ethical Hacker, who may not be as well-versed in the technology they posses, the Neophyte Hacker can prove to be an ace up your sleeve.

Root Dance

They are still trying to understand what is so great about gaining access as root. Thus, they will often seem baffled by the spontaneous eruption of dancing amongst their team members after they quietly ask a teammate "Hey, what do I do with this shell running as root?"

"Ineptus Maximus"

Inept Hacker

Summary

This is the "I don't know what the heck I'm doing" breed of Ethical Hacker. The Script Kiddie turned self-proclaimed security professional. This individual is lost but will neither realize nor admit it. They should have stayed in the fast food industry and worked their way from the fryer, to grill, to cashier and perhaps Assistant to the Regional Manager. But grandma told them they had skills with computers and somehow they managed to find themselves in the big, wide world of information technology. One never really knows how they worked their way into the profession but they did – they are freak accidents of nature. They are distant relatives of the Neophyte Hacker with one major difference, the Neophyte Hacker has potential and these little fellas and fellettes do not.

Identification

Although a prevalent breed, *Ineptus Maximus* can be extremely difficult to spot for the layperson; that is, until *Ineptus Maximus* has broken something. The good news? One only needs a modicum of technical and security knowledge to make a positive identification. For example, to ferret one out, simply watch the suspect during a technical exchange meeting with system developers. As the system owner rattles on with great pride about the E25k, SANs, load balancers, virtual application servers and their bridged public key infrastructure, *H. Ineptus Maximus* will listen intently with one eye half closed, puckered lips, and shake their head vigorously as if they have heard it all before.

Once the brief is over, they will walk into the data center, and with an impressive air of confidence begin their vulnerability assessment of your system. They will work for hours before finally calling you over to ask some pointed questions, like why do you have "hacker" tools on your system. Do not panic. Ten out of ten times, they will in fact have never actually plugged into your network. All this time they will have been scanning and discovering vulnerabilities on their own laptop.

One additional trait is their extremely limited focus, but take care not to misidentify them as *Limitus Oculus*. *Ineptus Maximus* will be focused only on what they know, such as pressing the big read "start" button on the latest fashionable security scanner. Push button security tools are one of the primary reasons for the success of this breed. Sadly, like a Biblical plague, they have infested many aspects of information security in the Government sector.

Handling Tips

Career counseling is the best way to work with these fellas. Someone needs to suck it up and tell them they are in the wrong career field, and that their talents

49

would better serve humanity elsewhere. Suggest the fast food industry but please do not push them into management. There are far too many that have strayed into this area and, like an infestation of plague carrying vermin, they are spreading their destructive bacterium throughout the IT and security departments of many organizations.

Now, if you are stuck with one these little fellas on your team, then you must recognize that the best case scenario is that your security assessments will be one big false negative – they will not find most of the things your customers should be concerned about. This of course will not impact your customers' ability to prove compliance with HIPAA, FISMA, PCI, and the like. However, their assessment of a system's security posture will be, simply put, a wild stab in the dark – which incidentally is what your system owners will wish to do to you after you let Ineptus Maximus break their system.

Root Dance

Root dance style has never been observed in the wild or even in captivity. They simply struggle to gain root level access to systems they themselves have installed, and so have never had a chance to develop a dance style.

Dissecting the Ethical Hacker
A guide for the Wine'n Cheese Crowd

"Solus Maximus"
The Lone Hacker

Summary

"Yippy Ki Ay" The old cowhands from the Rio Grande, learned to hack 'fore they learned to stand. *H. Solus Maximus*, like the ol' gunfighter of the West, has many variations: aged and wise, young and impetuous, and of course the wannabe that likes the sound of his own spurs a-jingling and a-jangling as he meanders through the data center. There are those that can knock over a domain controller a hundred hops away in the blink of an eye and those that "couldn'a hit the side of a rack a servers with a syn packet if they waz a'standing right in fron'a it."

Identification

There are two unique characteristics, which you will find in all the variations of *Solus Maximus*. The first is that they prefer the solo approach to ethical hacking. Very few are team players, choosing to ride the range of your data center all by their lonesome. Some may pick up a sidekick along the way – someone to fetch the vittles during late night hacking sessions or provide them with much needed praise after a particularly impressive gunfight with a fully patched server. But most will refuse to work with others and attempt to do all the work alone.

The second characteristic is that all their hacking is done from the hip. Without even the slightest preparation, "they'll a come into the data center a firing an'a fighting 'till your systems surrender." They are confident in what they know, and therefore in their minds they do not feel planning is worth their time. If they do any planning at all it will be brief and vague. "I'll meet you at noon to test your web application. Be ready."

Handling Tips

Caution is required as they have egos – more so relative to some of the other breeds – and they will take offense at the slightest insinuation that they did not do good work. Whether they are the Experienced and Wise or the Wannabe, they should be forced to take on a partner or two to take up the slack and fill in their knowledge gaps. Despite their skills, none of them can do it all alone. In fact, no breed of Ethical Hacker is adept at every technology you have in your data center. They are best in teams, and *Solus Maximus*, no matter how good he or she actually is, is no exception.

Root Dance

When they're done shooting those root terminals off of the fence post in your data center, they'll sling their laptop over their backs, hop up on their scooter, toss their hands limply over the handle bars, and ride off into the sunset singing:

I'm an old cowhand from the Rio Grande,

Dissecting the Various Breeds

And I learned to hack 'fore I learned to stand.

Under your racks I'll catch my Z's,
As my code makes a trail through your DMZ,
'cause I ride the range of your company.

Yippy I Ohhhhh Ki Ay, Yippy I Ohhhhh Ki Ay.

"Mongus"

Mongo Hacker

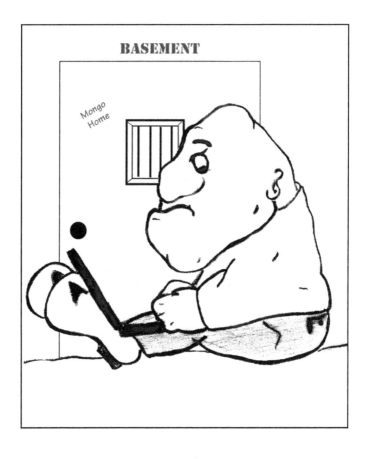

Summary

The brute of the ethical hacking world, this big fella is very good at one task and one task only. Some are good for simply smashing servers over the heads of system administrators, while others are application gurus, networking gurus, and so on. The point is, they know a technology or technique better than anyone.

Another unique characteristic is their lack of social skills. It is indeed, a dangerous game to play if one opts to release them on the Wine'n Cheese Crowd. They know how to find vulnerabilities but they absolutely do not know how to articulate themselves, "Mongo like test security. Mongo break in system, steal cookie. Hee, hee, hee." Yes, a dangerous game, indeed.

Identification

Lack of a neck is one obvious physical characteristic to look out for but be careful as it is not necessarily a definitive sign that you are, in fact, faced with a Mongo Hacker. The *Mongus* will be the individual that focuses all their ethical hacking efforts on one task and one task only.

When a *Mongus* comes in to conduct a vulnerability assessment on your system, they will spend hours, for example, scrutinizing your Windows operating systems – searching for every bug or misconfiguration in existence, and providing you valuable advice on how to reconfigure your Windows services and network in a secure manner. Then they will either not assess, or take only a cursory look at all the other components of your network or systems.

Handling Tips

As you may have guessed, these big guys are not going to provide a comprehensive security assessment beyond the one technology they know. So, using the above example, they may do a first-rate job of identifying all the security issues on your Windows operating system but they will not find, and therefore not tell you about, the insecure applications installed on those Windows servers, the vulnerabilities in your Unix systems, network devices or configurations, and so on.

It is best to keep these big guys in a cage deep in the bowels of the office. Release them only when you really want that *special* task performed and when they finish whip them with CAT5 cable until you can shepherd them back into their cage.

Root Dance

Stand safely back when you notice they are about to gain root access to a system. When the prompt changes from a $ to a # in their terminal window, *Mongus* will let out a shrill cry like a Yeti, often shattering nearby glass objects.

Presently, they will jump out of their seat and stomp around the data center like a giant child, laughing and smashing things with their oversized hands and ginormous feet.

"Trancendo"

Guru Hacker

Summary

Trancendo is one of the most technical Ethical Hackers to have evolved to date. They have at their disposal knowledge of every tool and technique ever invented to break into information systems. They transcend all others, to the point of being able to recall on command even the minutest syntactic detail for the most obscure security tool you can think of. They have achieved hacking nirvana.

Identification

Though their knowledge has surpassed most in the world of information security, they are not the type to scoff at the less technically minded nor will they flaunt their superior intellect. Rather, they often like to take people under their wings – having no problem sharing information. This is in contrast to many in the technical world that like to keep the non-technical (especially executives) thinking what they do is magic.

There are a couple methods for identifying the suspected *Trancendo*, that is, aside from the loose-fitted clothing, tranquil voice, and effortless way in which they bypass the multimillion dollar security protections you have just implemented in your organization. One technique is to casually drop in conversation something along the lines of, "I was scanning the network and noticed we had one NIC with multiple IPs. I tried pinging both IPs and it worked."

If you are not the type to be scanning networks (and this is obvious) then say that your son or daughter was doing this on your home network. The false Trancendo will look at you stupidly and say that you are mistaken. They will then go on to say something along the lines of not being able to have two systems using the same IP address because there will be a MAC address conflict – I know, blah blah blah – if none of this makes sense then do not worry. The true *Trancendo* will explain, in a soothing voice, how your son probably assigned multiple IPs to a single NIC card, and then go on to describe how the ARP protocol works. *Trancendo* will listen with clarity of thought, mind and body and provide clear, comprehensive answers to your questions.

Handling Tips

They are problem solvers, and need to be continuously working their minds. Boredom is their nemesis; you must keep them interested by involving them in challenging projects that provide real value to the security of the organization. But take care, as their constant thinking may sometimes causes them to be distracted from the task at hand, preventing them from finishing projects.

Though these fellas are highly technical, even the most gifted *Trancendo* should be teamed up with others because – joking aside – nobody knows everything. They do make excellent mentors, and you should use them often to train up new staff. But remember the boredom factor – do not pigeon-hole them into training all of your new team members or they will get bored and float away on their little cloud.

Root Dance

When a *Trancendo* achieves root, it is as if they have achieved nirvana. They will slowly levitate two feet off the ground, the clouds in the sky will part, and rays of sunshine will shine down upon their computer as the sweet voices of angels sing songs of praise and wonder.

UNDERSTANDING THEIR LANGUAGE

Intraspecies Communication

A study of *Haxorus ethicus's* communication methods can be overwhelming for one accustomed to the refined language of the Wine 'n' Cheese Crowd. Thankfully for the executive, only a cursory knowledge of their communication methods is required. Indeed, it would actually be dangerous for you to attempt a serious discourse with a member of the species using their native language. You risk looking foolish, and the *Haxorus ethicus* that sees you as a fool is apt to turn on you when you least expect it.

Haxorus ethicus has employed intelligent design principles to develop their unique form of communication specifically for the purpose of excluding all others from understanding them. Should their language become common place or understood by the Wine'n Cheese Crowd, the species would quickly adapt and begin a new evolutionary path of communication. They are worse than the French when it comes to tolerating others abusing their language, and harder to understand than a Shakespeare sonnet. While *you* may know that a "bare bodkin" is an unsheathed dagger they will consider you an @Rrog@n7 a$$ for stating this little fact.

The general term used to describe *Haxorus ethicus*'s method of communication is Leet speak, which is in fact a language that originally evolved from *Homo Technus*. Leet is a play on the word elite, which precisely illustrates the vast egos you are up against as a manager. When you learn a little about the mechanics of their language, you will notice that they misspelled "elite;" but do not make the mistake of believing they are illiterate buffoons, as this is merely a technique used to further obscure their means of communication.

The language's overriding characteristic is that it uses substitutions for the traditional letters that make up words. So, *"a"* becomes *"@"* or any other symbol that looks vaguely like the letter *"a"* can be used in its place. *"S"* becomes *"$"*, *"T"* becomes *"7"*, etc. A few popular terms to watch for are:

Hacker = h@x0r
Leet = 1337

Together they become *l337 h@x0r* or *elite hacker.* But beware. Do not become over confident, thinking this is simple to understand and akin to a child's game pulled from a cereal box. 1F u wR17E LoN9 5EN7enCEz U w1ll Be 7hOU9H7 4 BUfFoon. This is a minimalistic language – that is, the largest possible meaning in the fewest possible characters. Masters of the language can infuse great meaning in very few characters. For example, take this poem I found etched into stone tablets by my computer one morning.

-- ` !

An ode to my latest hack – God

Pronounced, "dash dash tic bang" in computer speak; and yes, this is the entire contents of the poem. It makes me cry every time I read it. What a beautiful statement about life, the universe and all that stuff. I had to rethink my place in this world when I found it.

The "bang" is a reference to the big bang, clearly, but the "dash dash tic" portion still keeps me up late at night wondering. These characters are often used in application hacking to comment out lines of code or generate errors. Why are they in a poem written by God? Did He have to break some other running program before the big bang, so he inserted these characters into the universe? Or was it the Devil that inserted the characters before the big bang? Did the Devil hack an older program of the universe and force a reboot? Was the big bang just a rebooting of an old system? Geez, are we all just malicious code running in God's data center? See what I mean, three unique symbols can possess a great deal of meaning.

Though they use Leet speak, some of the more brainy breeds in the *Haxorus Ethicus* community use modified or unique dialects. This is where things can start to get quite complex with their language. Indeed, substitutions can start to take the binary form using only 1's and 0's. So, "elite hacker" becomes:

01000111011011110110111101100100001000001001
01001101111011000100000110100001010

Other dialects use words that look strikingly similar to Standard English but understanding them when they are strung together to form sentences can be about as easy as trying to understand a West Country sheep herder reciting Stephen Hawking's unabridged theory of the universe while simultaneously downing a pint of ale – very difficult.

Consider the following simple phrase, "I injected a tic and pwnd the box". This translates to, "I entered a special character into an input field within the application, which failed to adequately process the character, and I gained privileged access to the server." Or consider, "I mod'ed the cookie and jacked an admin session," which translates to "I manipulated the value of a text file used by the website application to identify my access privileges and made the application think I was an administrator."

So, familiarize yourself with their mode of communication but remember, at no point should you *try to* engage *Haxorus ethicus* in a dialogue utilizing his native language. If you do find yourself attempting to exchange verbal or written banter with one using their native language then you must recognize that you are playing with a wild animal and all the dangers therein will follow. It is not likely to end well for you.

While it is important to have some basic understanding

of their method of intra-species communication, you should at no time have to trouble yourself to understand their language in great detail.

In short, your *Haxorus ethicus* must be domesticated and taught Standard English, or you must employ a translator in the form of a technical writer.

EXPLORING THEIR CULTURE
Learning About Their Likes and Dislikes

Learning a bit about the dress, games, habits and other cultural aspects of the ethical hacking world will vastly improve your understanding of the breed. And what better way to get up to speed then watch a quick movie or two? Now, the more ambitious executives will go on a movie watching binge, read the recommended books until their eyes bleed, parade back and forth in front of the mirror with some of the clothes, and fully explore the lifestyle. Others can simply use the information to dissect their subject, explore their psyche, and find out what makes them tick – in short, their likes and dislikes.

Television & The Movies

While the elders of the Ethical Hacking world have not officially recognized a set of must-watch cult movies for the Ethical Hacker, there are a few movies and T.V. programs with which you will want to familiarize yourself if you are going to survive as a leader on the mean streets of the l33t h@X-ng world. So upgrade your Netflix subscription, check out a few of these movies and commit to memory the characters, some quotes, and the gist of the plot. The good executive will even learn an odd tidbit about each movie to really shine (such as Will Smith passing on the lead role in the Matrix for a lead in Wild Wild West).

Incidentally, it was not easy culling the list of movies down to a manageable number. There are many good ones that had to be weeded out to avoid this becoming an encyclopedia of Hacker movies. Should I wish to self-publish this stuff, then too many pages will play havoc with my profit margins – and if I'm not careful I'll have to pay Amazon every time someone buys the book. Nevertheless, below is a nice solid foundation that will serve you well throughout your career – the really motivated should peruse the Internet to expand their hacking movie horizons.

Once more, this is a good time to top off your glass of wine before reading on.

The Matrix

A classic in the hacking world, you should study all three movies in this series closely. It is probably best if you watch each movie twice or even three times – until the characters, plot, and jargon really sink into your brain. I also recommend you browse Internet forums and other sites – do a Google search – to read the thoughts of others about the hidden meaning of this trilogy. But take care not to think yourself a Matrix guru as you will likely get caught. Most serious Ethical Hackers have seen it dozens, perhaps hundreds of times. In fact, many believe the Matrix to be our future and are preparing by staying current on nMap and hoarding all the milk, canned foods and black spandex.

A word of warning, never disparage this movie in the

company of Ethical Hackers. Always refer to it as a profound and original statement on the human condition with some pretty cool special effects. Your depth of knowledge about the Matrix trilogy will prove more valuable to understanding the Ethical Hacker than any real skill in information security you possess. It will also win you respect amongst the younger members of the breed.

War Games

"Would you like to play a game?" Heck yes! War Games is a must see movie from the pre-dawn Internet age, the 80's. Modern hacking culture can be traced back to this movie. War dialing, firewalls, brute-force attacks, password guessing, this one is a trip down memory lane for many in the world of technology. Study it and when you toss a quote or two into a conversation, do not forget to bash the attempted sequel, *War Games: The Dead Code*. Rumor has it Leonardo DiCaprio is producing a remake of the original. Matthew Broderick was a *Transcendo* (aka Guru Hacker) in the original but I do not think Leo could pull that off – he is more of a *Metrosexualus* I would say.

Hackers

"Hack the Planet!" Sweet Lord, this one is a classic stereotypical hacker movie that inspired a generation of teenage hackers. If you are 30-plus years old, I recommend you try to set aside the sheer cheesiness of it all and open yourself up to its profound commentary on the human condition. For example, it is almost eerie how, thematically speaking, common passwords have not changed throughout the generations. OK, it is not that profound - just watch the movie to better understand the childhood fantasies of the middle-aged hacker and to enjoy a few moments with a pre-cougar Angelina Jolie.

Most of the technical speak in *Hackers* bears no resemblance to reality. Be careful. Should you dare to attempt to mimic any of the movie's technical jargon in front of a real Ethical Hacker, you will likely be exposed as a BS artist. For example, most of the computers in the movie are Apple, yet at one point the l33t h@xors drool over Acid Burn's Pentium processor. True geeks like to point out this little tidbit (Apple machines do not use Intel processors). Believe it or not, it makes Ethical Hackers laugh.

Moving Right Along

OK, let's move things along as it is not my intention to play Roger Ebert to the hacking community. The above movies are a good start, but to really understand the Ethical Hacker you will need to suck it up and delve deeper. The below table lists a few must see movies and T.V. shows to help you understand the Ethical Hacker.

Blade Runner	What a warped vision of our future.
Sneakers	Cracking the code and running from the NSA. Thankfully, key loggers have reduced the need to use binoculars to record keystrokes.
Princess Bride	A classic with great lines that may crop up in conversations from time to time.
TRON	See the original as well as the newer release, *TRON: legacy*
Star Trek	Everything, movies, TV, watch it all.
Star Wars	The original triology – and if you must, the other three George made. Skip the cartoons and books.
Spinal Tap	There are a few that will never tire from quoting this movie – often making a poor attempt at a British accent.
Office Space	This is a cult classic that all must watch.
Lord of The Rings Trilogy	Watch the extended editions and all 400 hours of extra material – twice
Doctor Who	The younger generation of Ethical Hackers will think Doctor Who started in 2005, but you will do well to watch the old series – especially the ones with Jon Pertwee, Tom Baker, and Peter Davison as the...Dooooctoooor!
IT Crowd	When the British do television well, they really do it well. For Americans, we tend to have to force ourselves to stick with it until the humor 'clicks'

	but it's worth it. Watch the one about The Speech...actually, watch them all!
Red Dwarf	Another British program, and technically not really a must see for the Ethical Hacker unless you are European, but hey, watch this series anyway and the Black Adder series as well. They are both great learning aids for the development of spontaneous wit.
Battlestar Galactica	Start with the original series and see how far you get. Jump into the newer stuff if you find yourself getting hooked.
Buck Rogers	Do NOT forget to watch the intro for the first in the series.

CLARIFYING THEIR WRITTEN WORD

The Ethical Hackers' Canon

On the evolutionary timeline, it is still the dawn of the Ethical Hackers' literary development. But Philologist are starting to see the emergence of a definite Ethical Hacking Canon. This is to say, there is a collection of books that all Ethical Hackers should peruse if they want to live up to current cultural expectations.

The executive, on the other hand, need only concern themselves with a few works of literature. For the sake of simplicity, I've categorized the Canon into fiction and non-fiction. Fiction includes mostly technical books that are directly related to the profession of Information Security or Information Technology. Non-fiction are, well, those that are *not* fiction.

Presently, there is an intense and ongoing debate among l33t h@xors over which of two goliath works of literature should occupy the center of the non-fiction side of the Canon; that is, the gravitational core around which all other works in the Canon merely rotate. The two great works of literary genius are *Hitch Hikers Guide to the Galaxy* by Douglas Adams and the *Lord of the Rings* trilogy by J.R.R Tolkien. Tread carefully if you find yourself in the middle of a debate over which novel is at the true center of the Canon. Only those who have not only read these books but *lived* the associated lifestyle of a HHG or LoTR fanatic can expect to survive such a conversation intact.

While the center of the Canon remains hotly contested, nearly everyone in the profession worth their salt will agree that one cannot expect to be taken seriously in the world of information technology, let alone the world of information security, without having read both of these great works of literature. Together, they are to the Ethical Hacker Canon what Shakespeare is to the Western Canon. There never was a story of such woe, than this, the tale of thy manager of l33t h@xors who failed to read these works...oh, oh.

The sage manager will study both works in some detail. Many inside jokes in the world of Ethical Hacking will play on phrases, characters, ideas or other aspects of these classics. You should understand the Answer 42, if not the question, or the reasons why everyone is going crazy over a silly ring. Or why Altavista named their online translator Babelfish. It is imperative that you pick up on these references in conversation or you risk being an Ethical Hacking outcast.

You may be thinking a visit to Wikipedia or a quick search for movies on IMDB will save you some potentially unnecessary reading. While this is an admirable strategy, it is not recommended in this case. You may get away with watching the extended version of Peter Jackson's LoTR but, sadly, there are no decent movie adaptations for Hitchhikers. If you rely on the sparse and poorly done T.V. and movie adaptations for HHG, then you will quickly get yourself in trouble.

Read at least the first three in the Hitch Hiker series to fully appreciate Marvin the depressed android, the sweet intensity of a Pan Galactic Gargalblaster, the joyous sounds of Vogon poetry, the significance of 42 and the many other humorous aspects of the book (yes these examples are all humorous to Ethical Hackers).

Moving on to the nonfiction portion of the Canon, one quickly finds that the market is saturated with l33t h@xor books. One simple search on the term "hacking" at your favorite on-line bookstore will produce an overwhelming list of results. There is an overabundance of hacking books out there but you will be happy to know that it is not necessary for you (as a member of the Wine'n Cheese Crowd) to read them.

What is more important is the *appearance of having read* these and other non-fiction books within the Canon. And, the best approach to successfully achieving an appearance of Ethical Hacking well-read-ed-ness is to simply decorate your office with a selection of hacking and general technology books. Think of yourself as an actor or actress and these books as props for your stage, i.e. your office.

First in your collection you will want anything written by Bruce Schneier. A great strategy is to have his *Applied Cryptography* book casually lying about as if you need to reference information on cryptographic algorithms on a fairly regular basis.

However, be careful to whom you flash it around because you may be asked questions that go well beyond the title and introduction. Another author's books you will want lying about is Kevin Mitnik's. He is a bad guy turned good – and folks in Information Security seem to think this is cool; his sordid past gives him a bit of a James Dean edge I suppose. Crime has clearly paid for him.

Next, fill your office bookshelves with inane titles like *Ninja Hacking*, *Cyber Warrior from Hell*, and *Hack Naked*. The more asinine the book titles the better. Place these books strategically around your office, under your chair and on your desk. To compliment your collection, add as many pure technology books as you can afford. Books about programming in Ruby and Python are particularly good, but also books on Linux, Windows, networking and other technical subjects. Toss in a really obscure one like something on femtocell technology. Many of these you can find at a library sale for a buck or two – don't forget to take off the call number sticker.

Though you will likely never read beyond the titles of these books, it is important that they look used and abused. Nothing says you are a bluffer more than a crisp, clean book with pages that still stick together when the book is opened. Spend some quality time dog-earring your collection. A nice trick is to put a few in your dryer on tumble dry for about an hour. Lastly, always keep your copy of *Dissecting the Ethical Hacker* nearby but out of sight! These little fellas and fellettes might not like the thought of you studying them like a lab rat.

EXAMINING THEIR WORK

Hacking Their Way Through Your Enterprise

Socrates on Ethical Hacking

To truly understand the Ethical Hacker, you must take a journey across the river Styx and into the first level of hell (I know, I'm confusing my Greek mythology with Dante, but stay with me and things will become clear...ish). Once across, snake your way through crowds of howling shades clawing at your flesh until you finally arrive at a non-descript little Pub, The Devil's Toenail[2].

Take a deep breath and bravely enter the Pub. Push passed the condemned drinking their way through eternity and head towards the back where you will find an unimposing little man in a toga, sipping a pint of ale, and chatting casually with a gaggle of grey hat hackers. The man is Socrates, the famous Greek philosopher. Do not be frightened, he was not banished to hell for bad deeds – unlike the grey hat hackers gathered around him. You must ask Socrates for his help. You must ask him, "What the hell does an Ethical Hacker actually do?"

Never one to be direct, he will immediately fire back at you a serious of insightful questions and you will find yourself quickly lost in a dialogue about the meaning of terms you previously took for granted. Dissecting each and every word, Socrates will ensure everyone listening understands the assumptions and meanings of words

---

[2] Pubs are typically named after the body parts of royalty so I assume the convention is similar in Hell.

before they start tossing them around in conversation.

He will do this because the meaning of various words, or what people think they mean, dictates the direction and outcome of a conversation. As you listen intently to this little barefoot, toga wearing man, sipping ale in hell and clarifying the world of ethical hacking it may cross your mind how amazing it is that a two thousand five hundred year old methodology, that is, simply clarifying terminology, still works today.

When it comes to the work of the Ethical Hacker, you will hear terms like vulnerability assessment and penetration testing casually tossed around in conversations, usually in a manner that will make you frightened to ask, "What the heck are you talking about?" As you move from one gaggle of Ethical Hackers to the next, you will find that everybody you meet is an expert but no two experts' opinions about what exactly it is they are expert at doing will be the same.

As an exercise, put down your glass of wine and type *penetration testing methodology* into your favorite search engine. Spend a few moments sifting through the gobbledygook that is returned. Try to figure out what blind penetration testing is and how it differs from double-blind penetration testing or red teaming. Figure out what a reversal or tandem penetration test is without going completely insane. If you still have the mental capacity, delve into the concept of a vulnerability assessment and figure out what exactly is involved in one and who performs them.

If you find sifting through all this nonsense quite comical, then congratulations, you are beginning to understand these little fellas. I mean really, "crystal box" penetration testing? Someone is having a serious laugh.

The Ethical Hacker lexicon is clearly the result of sixteen year olds – either physically or mentally – who have spent far too many evenings watching T.V. or playing video games with their online clans when they should have been out with real girls or drinking beer from a pony keg in the bed of a pickup truck parked on a mountainous back road...er...not that I'd know what that feels like.

While many in the industry have a solid grasp of the concepts, few have a solid grasp on how to describe these concepts or document their work in a way that benefits an organization's security program. They use their in-depth technical knowledge and sophisticated security tools (despite the unsophisticated names) to dissect your organization's systems. They then attempt to articulate their findings in a report that often reads like a Neanderthal with a brain injury wrote it using a twig dipped in ink and wedged between their toes. "Me test, you screwed."

The Evil Threats

Though this may seem self evident, in the interest of clarifying terms, Ethical Hackers are the *ethical* versions of the evil people that are out to get us. To understand the Ethical Hacker, we need to explore the dark side of the business, the people they are protecting you from and, at times, simulating. These people are called threats.

Threats exploit vulnerabilities to achieve their particular goals. What are their goals? How vulnerable are you and how likely is it that the threats will successfully exploit you? If they do exploit a vulnerability in your system, what will this mean for your business? Which protections should you put in place and what vulnerabilities should you mitigate to get the most bang for your buck?

There. That was a quick, to-the-point, course in risk management. All you have to do is answer those questions for your organization.

Great business leaders know how to ask and answer the right questions – this is true, I know, because I read it somewhere – and these are the questions your security program should be asking. The Ethical Hacker will help you answer them. To learn how they do it, we must delve into the threats, i.e. the reason we need security programs in the first place.

When thinking about threats of the human kind, think about motivation. When you do, you will realize there are a vast amount of reasons why people wish to gain access to your systems and information or to do you damage. The insider stealing your secret formula, the individual out to save the world by taking your pet shop website down, the bored teenager out to make a name for themselves at your expense, and so on.

We simplify by lumping everyone into one category— *threats* – but never forget that the term is plural, and like a Baskin Robbins ice cream of old, they come in a thousand flavors and have very different objectives.

But a thousand is unmanageable, so here is a list of the main categories of threats, of which every business leader should be aware.

Hacktivists
: These folks are motivated by an ideology. Think the tree huggers and PETA gone cyber or the currently fashionable Anonymous, who think hacking can right all the worlds wrongs (in reality they just need an excuse to hack and any seemingly altruistic motive will do).

Cyber Criminals
: Just like the flesh and blood world of crime, cyber criminals are usually after money. This category includes the purse snatching-type cyber criminals to the more sophisticated jewel thieves of the cyber world.

Examining Their Work

Cyber Criminals /
Organized

These folks deserve a category to themselves as this group represents the organized criminals that have jumped online – La Cyber Nostra. They are well-funded, well-organized, and no longer interested in transporting bootlegged liquor across the border. Like multinational corporations, they are diversifying their evil little business model.

Cyber Terrorists

Those motivated by politics or ideology – finding ways to use computers to facilitate their agenda because they are too weak to engage in full-scale war. This isn't just strapping a DoS-bomb to a TCP packet or hacking from mountain caves – they are not necessarily cavemen with computers.

Corporate Spies

Those out to steal the corporate crown jewels for economic gain or sabotaging a competitor. Maybe a one-off insider or a corporate or state sponsored group.

Cyber Warriors

Rambo with a computer. As ol' Carl Von Clausewitz stated, "War is the continuation of politics by other means." These folks use some of the other means. They are professional war fighters going after targets of tactical or strategic importance to achieve a military objective. You may not be the Pentagon, but remember that many believe civilian targets are just as valid as military targets in times of war.

Black Hat Hackers

Rogue hackers creating virus, worms and other malicious hacks who are motivated by misguided curiosity, a warped sense of humor, hacker fame, boredom or money. This is also a general term for the bad guys. Recall the old western movies where the bad guys wore a black cowboy hat while the good guys wore white.

Grey Hat Hackers These folks are really Black Hat Hackers that think they are doing good deeds. They are the hackers that, for example, hack illegally into corporations to "show them" how vulnerable they are to attack. Supposedly all in the name of a greater good, but in actuality, they are usually frustrated security professionals out to make a name for themselves or who have gotten carried away and strayed out of the scope of their role.

Spammers One of the original threats from the early days of the Internet, they are motivated by making money. This includes those that like to use your systems to spread adware as well as junk email.

Script Kiddies Those with limited hacking abilities and who are typically motivated by a desire to show off to their friends or impress a girl. They are still learning how to find their hacking feet and therefore rely on other people's hacking tools, scripts, etc. Incidentally, this is an excellent derogatory term to throw at an Ethical Hacker that has angered you.

Foreign Intelligence Motivated by international politics, these are state sponsored spies that play their spy

Services

games online. Also considered Advanced Persistent Threat (APT) because they are pretty advanced, persistent as heck, and definitely a threat. Again, remember civilian targets are fair game to these fellas and fellettes. Also remember, though fashionable and useful for marketing security products, they are not the only threat.

Insider Threat

Any of the above threats can also be an insider threat, i.e., working as a trusted insider at the target organization. This category also includes the stupid user, mistakes by developers, accidents, and other such acts or misuses of information resources by insiders.

Ethical Hackers, Auditors, Security Managers, and Other Security Professionals

Often overlooked, these folks are a threat because the less skilled in the group can misrepresent risk, fail to identify actual risk, force an organization to focus resources in the wrong area, and generally make folks run around with their heads cut off - they divert attention from real solutions to real risk. In some organizations, the security program would be considered an Advanced Persistent Threat if it were not for the advanced requirement.

Vulnerability Assessments

It takes much more than technical prowess or a two day hacking boot camp in some exotic city to be good at finding all of the many colors and flavors of vulnerabilities that exist in an organization. *Knowing* that vulnerabilities exist on systems, in business processes, in physical security protections, etc. is one thing – discovering them is quite another.

Being good at discovering them requires the Ethical Hacker to be knowledgeable and creative like a virtuoso pianist. While it is easy to sit at the piano and make noise, it is not easy to make music. In the ethical hacking world, it is easy to press the "go" button on a vulnerability scanner, but only the best Ethical Hacker, like the pianist, knows how to perfectly blend the science of their instrument with the art of making music.

You know the "who", so let's discuss the "what", "why" and "how" of a first-rate vulnerability assessment, starting with the why. And the why is a real shocker. The reason for conducting a vulnerability assessment is ...drum roll please...to *identify vulnerabilities*. Well, that and to get your compliance box checked for the auditors, but let's focus on the former.

You may ask, "Why do we want to identify vulnerabilities? Isn't ignorance bliss?" Well yes ignorance *is* bliss, like the deer blissfully slurping up a mouthful of refreshing early morning water from a sweet babbling brook just before a hunter blows its head off. Ignorance will not do in the age of information. Organizations cannot necessarily purchase insurance to *insure* their way out of cyber related risks. For example, damaged brands are not going to be repaired by an insurance payout.

We identify vulnerabilities so that folks can fix them before the bad guys and gals can exploit them. A vulnerability assessment is like the physical exam your doctor subjects you to every once in a while; that is, the Ethical Hacker puts on the rubber gloves, bends the system over, and goes in up to the elbow for a real in-depth look at the health of the system.

What does going in up to the elbow look like? It means the Ethical Hacker goes into the assessment with a solid understanding of the system architecture,

The scope of the assessment is based on what the threat sees – not what the auditors see.

trust relationships, the technology, the business processes, the data, the users, the administrators, and the mission that the system supports. It means putting aside internal politics and looking at all aspects of a system, even if compliance boundaries or organizational boundaries are crossed. The scope of the assessment is based on what the threat sees – not what the auditors see or the system owners and administrators want you to see.

As you know, systems are interconnected and interdependent. In fact, it is difficult to even define what a system actually is or where one system starts and the next begins within an organization's I.T. infrastructure. Therefore, the Ethical Hacker must have access to anything and everything that might impact the security of the system *if* the goal is to identify vulnerabilities.

But conducting a first-rate vulnerability assessment does not end with access to system information.

Many systems are too complex for any single person to understand every aspect of them, and therefore, a well-resourced, well-rounded and well-led team of Ethical Hackers is required to truly identify the vulnerabilities on a system. Well-resourced means taking a "toolbox" approach to conducting a vulnerability assessment; using the right tool for the job – not a one-size-fits-all approach, which unfortunately is all the rage today. The right tool may be custom, commercial or publically available and appropriate for the task at hand.

Well-rounded means that the team has the right mix of business, security and technical skills: web application specialists, networking gurus, operating system specialists, storage and database specialists, wireless specialists, mobile devices wizards, mission specialists, and business gurus are just a few of the skill sets a team will need.

Well-led means that the team is lead by someone who understands your business and knows how to lead technical people; how to pull them together when they are often more comfortable on their own, how to effectively direct their efforts, and how to extract the best out of them. It also means the leader knows how to staff, resource and deploy a vulnerability assessment team.

Vulnerabilities can exist anywhere, and are not necessarily technical in nature. And most will never be found by that automated security solution you

A low-quality risk assessment will always destroy any real value the organization may have obtained from a high-quality vulnerability assessment.

purchased from the sexy red head at the last security conference you attended. If your team of Ethical Hackers does not find them, then you can bet someone else eventually will.

A high-quality vulnerability assessment is not the end of the story. All the work of the Ethical Hacker is wasted if it is not used by knowledgeable risk assessment professionals who consider all the variables often left out of a vulnerability assessment; such as, cost of mitigating vulnerabilities, mission objectives and priorities, and mitigating factors outside the scope of the vulnerability assessment.

A low-quality risk assessment will always[3] destroy any real value the organization may have obtained from a high-quality vulnerability assessment. The output of a low-quality risk assessment is often a laundry list of "fix-it" items tossed over the wall of information security and onto the field of the system owner. You fix them but the company gets hacked anyway.

---

[3] If the goal is a check box for compliance then do not bother with the high-quality vulnerability assessment.

Penetration Testing & Red Teams

Blind, double-blind, crystal, white, black, grey, red, tandem – when it comes to the concept of penetration testing there are quite a few confused people slipping and sliding on puddles of verbal diarrhea spewed across the floor of the security profession. Those that provide penetration testing services and those that receive the services have widely disparate ideas about the "who, what, and why" of this type of security assessment.

Often, the work some do under the guise of a penetration test is argued by others to be more of a vulnerability assessment. And there are always arguments about who does penetration testing better – the cyber security world is not immune to the phenomena of the intellectual snob as you have already learned from *Egomaniacnus technum*.

To understand these concepts, you should first understand that neither a penetration test nor its cousin, the red team exercise, is a vulnerability assessment. To gain a comprehensive understanding of your risk, you need to perform regular vulnerability assessments supplemented by regular high quality penetration tests and continuous red team exercises. If you are forced to choose between these three options, then go with the vulnerability assessment every time.

OK, now that we have that out of the way, lets delve into

these two types of security assessments.

To begin to understand the concept of penetration testing or red team exercises – and these are two distinct types of security assessment – we must use the lessons we learned from Socrates and define the terms. Understanding the terms and concepts will help you spot the bluffers, help you effectively direct your security resources, and help you maximize the benefit from your Ethical Hackers' efforts.

The National Institute of Standards and Technology (NIST) defines red team exercise as:

"An exercise, reflecting real-world conditions, that is conducted as a simulated adversarial attempt to compromise organizational missions and/or business processes..."

The Committee on National Security Systems has something similar for red teams:

"A group of people authorized and organized to emulate a potential adversary's attack or exploitation capabilities against an enterprise's security posture..."

Both of these organizations define a penetration test as:

"A test methodology in which assessors, typically working under specific constraints, attempt to circumvent or defeat the security features of an

information system."

Simply put, what we are talking about are controlled simulations of threats. Blind, double-blind, blindfolded, crystal, grey, black, white, pink, purple, Ninja-style, no matter what Ethical Hackers wish to call them, simulating threats is at the heart of it all.

Vulnerability assessments are used to identify vulnerabilities and help organizations tighten up security while penetration tests and red team exercises are the one opportunity you will have to look at your systems and organization through the eyes of your enemy. These techniques provide you the ability to test the effectiveness of all that work you put into your defenses before your adversaries test it for you.

The difference between the two types of adversarial-based testing is that the red team operates under more real-world conditions,

This is your opportunity to see your systems and organization through the eyes of your enemy.

i.e., operational environments, whereas a penetration test typically has a reduced scope and tighter rules of engagement. Penetration testing may be performed in operational or even non-operational environments, while red team exercises are not performed in labs or development environments.

Another difference is that red teams, perceived as the special forces of the ethical hacking world, usually stop once they have reached their objective. Like playing King of the Hill, once they find a way to the top, it's game over. They stop because this type of an assessment tends to be directed towards assessing the defense and monitoring capability of an organization rather than identifying every unique vector possible to reach the objective. On the other hand, Penetration testers will typically reset themselves once they have achieved an objective, and start with new assumptions or test a different vector – which incidentally is why some consider penetration testing simply a vulnerability assessment on steroids.

Penetration tests, typically, are much more controlled and comprehensive than a red team exercise – at least those that are done well. They are a more comprehensive assessment with respect to their scope because they tend to be more focused on a specific area of the organization, and do not (or should not) stop until the timer ticks down to zero. The Ethical Hackers use the time allotted for the testing to identify every possible path to the objective.

For example, malicious user testing could be considered a form of penetration testing. This is where the Ethical Hacker starts an assessment (say for a critical web application on your network) from the perspective of one of the users of that application. They then attempt to escalate their privileges either horizontally (gain access as another user on the system) or vertically (gain access as someone with more privileges, such as an administrator). Sometimes the Ethical Hacker only uses the resources available to the role of the specific insider they are simulating, but often they are allowed to introduce malicious tools using the same methods a threat would, such as tools from a flash drive or CD. As an aside, these techniques are great ways to find flaws in application logic or business processes.

As mentioned, both penetration testing and red team exercises provide an opportunity for your Ethical Hackers to see your organization and systems through the eyes of the threats targeting you. Viewing systems in this way is quite revealing, as often, small vulnerabilities when chained together turn out to be like the little door at the heart of Alice's tree – they open up a whole new world.

Watch out for the charlatans.

If penetration tests and red team exercises are a simulation of threats, then from our discussion on threats, you should recognize that most Ethical Hackers are *not* going to be able to realistically simulate threats. Now, many Ethical Hackers reading this will cry foul as I've just bruised their fragile egos. But let's think about threats again for a moment, while they lick their wounds.

You have to protect your organizations from a variety of threats because you do not get to choose which ones are going to come after you. Threats are not a single entity, but a variety of folks with a variety of resources, unique motivations, varying objectives, and varying degrees of ethics – starting with no ethics at all.

Threats are after something, and it is rarely a terminal window running as root. Ethical Hackers are, generally speaking, hyper-focused on the minutia of the penetration test or red team exercise – that is, the latest fashionable tools and techniques to gain access to that terminal window running as root. Too frequently, they are removed from any real understanding of the threats they are simulating. Tests are driven by the skills or whims of the Ethical Hackers rather than a solid understanding of the threats, their motivations, and their objectives. Many threats do not need root to achieve their objective.

The real challenges to simulating threats are legal, ethical, monetary, and time. Ethical Hackers, and most organizations that provide ethical hacking services, do not have legal authority or the resources to simulate many of threats organizations face.

Think about it, who really has the resources and time to simulate anything but an advanced, minimally funded, threat? Ethical Hackers are not like the determined criminal, who has a suitcase full of cash, all the time in the world, no concern for the law, and a network of evil cohorts. They are not going to be able to truly simulate the threats sponsored by evil corporations, criminal organizations, or nation states.

Understanding what you are receiving from their services is important. Be skeptical of those Ethical Hackers that focus on technology or techniques rather than focusing on the threats. Never trust someone who beats away on your systems for a few days with a popular penetration testing tool, and then claims everything is "all secure". While this will please the auditors and give you a warm fuzzy feeling, it will do nothing for the security of your organization. Anybody that thinks a penetration test or red team exercise can be performed with a single tool in a day, week, or month is, as the British say, "having a laugh." Good work takes time.

The Tools & Toys

Picture, if you will, a spring afternoon. The moon roof in the limousine allows the warm, fragrant air to gently waft inside and fill your senses. With the Gundlach Bundachu Vineyard in the rearview mirror and a case full of Gewurztraminer in the trunk, you head to the next destination. The picturesque scenery along California State Highway 12 scrolls past your window. You take another sip of your Gewurzt, remarking on its nice legs. Suddenly, you are overtaken with and intense sense of anticipation and joy. The driver has turned into the long, rose lined driveway of the next vineyard on your tour. "I wonder," you think with anticipation, "what wonderful selection of wines they will have at this one?"

Now, with the same sense of anticipation and joy, let us take a tour through the valley of the Ethical Hacker and sample some of the many tools and toys they use to test the security of your systems. Indeed, many of their tools have just as interesting, if not more interesting, names as some of the wines you love. Instead of Stag's Leap or Barefoot Vineyards, the Ethical Hacker has BurpSuite, Maltego, Kali, and hacking tools from vintners named The Cult of the Dead Cow.

OK. Perhaps this tour of the tools and toys of the Ethical Hacker will not have quite as nice legs as that Gewurztraminer, but cut me some slack. I'm trying to help you relate to what is likely not a very interesting subject for you. Thankfully, a comprehensive review of the tools and toys of the Ethical Hacker is not really necessary for you to understand them. What is necessary is that you have a solid sense of the types of tools, the techniques and, importantly, what they need to perform high quality security assessments for you.

Let's drive on. To help you get your head around their tools and toys, think search, scan, and exploit. Say it to yourself, "search, scan, exploit." Again, "search, scan, exploit, oh my!" All of their tools, for the most part, can be lumped into one of these categories. That is, tools used to search out target systems or people and scan those targets for vulnerabilities. Or tools to exploit vulnerabilities or built-in functionality and dig a foothold onto your systems.

Let us start with searching. Bad guys, and therefore the Ethical Hackers, need to find their victims somehow. To facilitate this stage of their hacking process, a vast suite of commercial and publically available, i.e. free, software is available to assist them. Some of it is highly specialized – geared towards just finding mail servers, web servers, or weak services exposed to the Internet, while other tools (typically the ones you have to pay for) try to be everything to everyone.

There are hundreds, perhaps even thousands of tools, to help Ethical Hackers find targets in just about every environment that organizations can architect. But one common, everyday, run-of-the-mill, household tool will do the trick and help me illustrate my point. Yep. The good ol' fashioned Internet search engine, i.e. Google, Yahoo, Altavista and friends.

While you are trying to find information about the best tasting rooms in Napa Valley or the little know wine region around Murphy's California (tip: try Four Winds Cellars if you are in the Murphy's area), Ethical Hackers are using that search engine to find *targets*.

Google for example has a nifty little feature called *search operators* to assist their users in narrowing down a search. For example "intitle" or "inurl" operators let you search just the title of web documents, or for terms that appear in the website's address, i.e. the URL.

To find places to try new wine you might type into Google something like:

INTITLE:sierra,foothills,four,winds,cellars

But the Ethical Hacker will look for web pages on the Internet that look something like:

INTITLE:"Nessus Scan Report"

Anything that responds to this – and it often works on internal corporate search engines too – will present interesting results to someone that is looking for vulnerable targets. Incidentally, Nessus does not refer to the little trickster in Greek Mythology who tried to steal Hercules's wife and was shot through the heart with an arrow. The name has been appropriated for use with a popular commercial vulnerability assessment tool.

Often times, less adept security professionals will store Nessus reports in places where they should not be stored. This not only makes it easy for folks in the Wine'n Cheese Crowd to access the little reports and review the security of their organization, but it also makes it easy for bad guys to access these little reports and exploit all the problems others have conveniently discovered for them.

The use of search engines does not stop there. Indeed, Ethical Hacking is an art as much as a science. If you do not agree, then tell me it wasn't creativity that came up with this little search:

INURL:updown.php | INTEXT:"Powered by PHP Uploader Downloader"

The results from this search will return a host of systems, all running a program that is offering an attacker the ability to upload their evil little software.

The algorithms that companies like Google use to search and index information available on the Internet are guarded tighter than any government secrets. This is because they are doing something magical: they are getting your systems to tell Google everything about themselves. It is as if Oprah Winfrey helped write some of this software – because boy does it work well. The Oprah algorithm will convince your systems to tell all.

The Oprah algorithm will convince your systems to tell all their dirty little secrets to the world.

Many vulnerable systems broadcast or return signatures that search engines, crawling networks, locate and index. Ethical Hackers, like the bad guys, try to find these little leaks before the bad guys do. And even the less skilled can perform thousands of complex searches for a vast variety of vulnerable services and applications, using tools such as Maltego. But tools like Maltego do not know what terms are important to you, only a skilled Ethical Hacker can customize the toys to find your leaks.

Finding targets is merely one third of the equation. The next step for the Ethical Hacker is to check their targets for vulnerabilities. Again, there is a seemingly endless amount of tools to assist them in finding vulnerabilities in just about every technology that humans have ever thought of. Remember back a few chapters? System engineers and developers use tools to build and create while the Ethical Hacker builds tools to break those creations.

When the Ethical Hacker has found the house, i.e. one of your corporate servers, that they want to break into, then they need tools and toys to help them. Nmap is perhaps the most common tool used to jiggle the door knobs and try the windows on hundreds of houses a minute. Nmap will even find those secret doors you thought nobody knew about. It will knock on the door and pretend to be everything from the post man to a singing candy gram until someone pokes their head out and answers.

But even if the door to your house is not open, tools like Nmap – in the right hands – can still peer through that window where you forgot to draw the curtains shut. Peering inside often reveals the types of technologies your organization is using, information about your organization and other nifty little tidbits that help bad guys construct attacks against you.

Vulnerabilities come in many shapes, sizes, and colors. Why? Because people and technology come in many shapes, sizes and colors. Technically speaking, our offices and data centers are more cosmopolitan than London, Paris, *and* New York all put together in a bag, shaken, and poured out onto Las Vegas Boulevard. Mobile devices, network devices, wireless devices, web applications, desktop applications, operating systems...you get the idea. Each of these technologies offers a bad guy a way into your organization.

The Ethical Hacker uses an array of crazy techniques and a vast suite of security tools to find holes in all those technologies. Tools with names like BurpSuite, AngryIP, Kismet, CAIN, Zed Attack Proxy, DirBuster..., and the list goes on ad infinitum. If it has been invented, then the Ethical Hacker has invented a way to find its weaknesses. And so have the bad guys.

And once they find those weaknesses, they pounce like Tigger of Winnie-the-Pooh fame. "Whoo, whoo, whoo, whooooo!" The nature of their pounce depends on the vulnerability they are exploiting. For example, if they want to launch a remote exploit across a network, then Metasploit is a popular tool. Its popularity is due to it being a first-rate tool and, most importantly, a free tool. Remember, Ethical Hackers cannot afford to fund an army of evil software developers, or purchase exploit kits off the black market for a few hundred thousand dollars.

To up their game, they have banded together on numerous open source and free software development projects, and the result is an impressive suite of free tools that are very effective – some more so than others. Metasploit is one of the more effective ones. Incidentally, as a sage member of the Wine'n Cheese Crowd, you will instantly recognize the benefits of these free tools. Yep, Ethical Hackers are cheap dates.

111

Launching remote exploits is not the only way into a system. They use tools like John the Ripper to crack passwords, they spider your websites looking for information, they use programming languages named after snakes, and one of the newest cool set of tools in their arsenal are the Pwn Plug, Raspberry Pi, ODroid, and other computers the size of a credit card which can turn your closed wired network into an open wireless network that they can then access while sipping a double latte in a comfortable high backed chair at a nearby Starbucks.

But if all the tools in their little toy chest fail to produce results, then they simply call up your administrators and ask them for an account. "Yeah, I'm a new employee in the Walla Walla, Washington office but I can't seem to access our SSH server…"

If you do not think this could possibly work, then go back a few chapters and read about Kevin Mitnik. The best Ethical Hackers are not necessarily the most technical, just like all the threats you face are not evil technical geniuses. Even the infamous *Ineptus Maximus* can put together a malicious program and send it to your employees. Only one of them needs to fall for the trick, and then he or she is inside your network. But it is creativity combined with some technical skills that leads to successful attacks.

One final point needs to be made on the subject of tools

because there seems to be a misconception amongst some in the Wine'n Cheese Crowd about *what* Ethical Hackers need to find all those nasty vulnerabilities on systems. Many unfortunate souls believe that a single security tool can do the trick. The Ethical Hacker need simply press a button and presto! All the vulnerabilities in your organization present themselves in a nicely bound report.

In fact, nothing could be further from the truth. While there are many security tools that claim to be able to do everything at the press of a button, the reality is they will not find everything. They are not even going to find *all* of the "low-hanging-fruit" in many cases. It is not that automated tools do not have a place in this world, it is that you need to use them with eyes wide open and with an understanding of what they are doing and not doing for the security of your organization. As a Great Indian Chief once said to Ben Franklin, "each thing has its use, and whatever the use, that use it should be put to." (Granted, the thing the Chief was talking about was alcohol, and he was making his apologies for consuming a bit too much the previous evening, but the concept translates.) Many techniques for identifying or exploiting vulnerabilities require specialized tools or techniques, and do not lend themselves to a single automated solution. Let the Ethical Hackers put their tools to use.

There are many first-rate commercial and publically

available (free) security tools, and most of them are developed to perform a specific set of tasks for a set of technology. The best Ethical Hackers use a toolbox approach, that is, they select the best tool for the task at hand. Never trust the security of your system to someone who bases their vulnerability assessment or penetration test on a single tool. These individuals are simply doing the minimum to please the security auditors. Remember, the bad guys are human beings that are constantly thinking outside the box and using their creativity.

SOME FINAL THOUGHTS
AND A WORD OF WARNING
Putting a Cork in It.

Today, the biggest threat to the security of many organizations is *their very own security program*. Too many security programs are based entirely on automation and auditors, with the end result being a target-rich environment for threats. Putting your faith in a compliance program is like building your house out of straw. It may keep some of nature's elements out, and probably looks beautiful, but the wind and the wolf will eventually blow it down, and you will be eaten.

Understandably, many corporate leaders, especially technology leaders, do not know what security services they truly need from Ethical Hackers — or others in the security profession for that matter. Leaders are often bombarded with solutions to problems they do not fully understand, or offered services they do not need (a week long penetration test in lieu of a vulnerability assessment is not going to do anything for the security of your organization). Folks are forced to chase fashions rather than to truly understanding their own strengths and weaknesses.

The danger of not understanding your Ethical Hackers, and security professionals in general, is an ill-informed executive basing critical corporate decisions on bad information. The result is typically a misallocation of corporate resources, misallocation of ethical hacking resources (obtaining little value from their endeavors), and the misallocation of corporate resources to track and chase every little "finding" identified by an Ethical Hacker or – Heaven help us – a high-speed automated security testing tool.

All the while the automated tools and multitude of auditors have not discovered the real risk to your organization. Many are building a brick wall in their front yard while the back and side fences are filled with holes they do not even know about because they are not looking. But the bad guys are looking for the holes, finding them, and crawling into your yard.

There are real threats out there that want something from your organization. Sometimes they will merely be a nuisance, like a fly buzzing your face, and sometimes they will cause serious damage to your organization or its people. If you believe others will protect you, then consider what White House Press Secretary Jay Carney said about one ongoing threat:

> *"I can tell you that we have repeatedly raised our concerns at the highest levels about cyber theft with senior Chinese officials including in the military and we will continue to do so."*

If you believe raising concerns will protect you, then, well, I'm reminded of an old Robin Williams joke about an English police officer chasing a criminal. The police man shouts as he runs, "Stop! Or I'll say stop again!" Marketing brochures, pretty reports, and empty words are not going to protect you – a solid and *continuously tested and improved* defense will protect you.

The services a well-managed group of Ethical Hackers provides can be extremely valuable to the security of your organization – beyond simply satisfying compliance needs. But you need to manage them, and you need to recognize the charlatans, because there are many.

Recall how I unashamedly laid out a few caricatures of Ethical Hackers, placing them comfortably into nice little cubbyholes. The little portraits (breeds) were created not just to amuse you but to illustrate a few characteristics that I am sure many of you who have worked in the area of information technology, especially information security, have observed over the years.

The breeds illustrate the differing approaches to information security and technology, which are present in many Ethical Hackers. Indeed some folks may cycle through many of these profiles throughout their career or perhaps even throughout a single day.

> **Destroius Maximus** – the person who uses every tool in their toolbox on your systems and usually breaks things.

> **Me'us Abouticus** – the narcissist who is only interested in showing off their own abilities or trying out the neat new technique they recently learned in some training course or book.

> **Theoreticus Maximus** – the individual that has read every book about information security, probably has multiple

degrees and certifications, but really is not a "doer". They are not practical.

Limitus Oculus – the hyper focused Ethical Hacker who will not do a comprehensive security assessment because they become fixated on one component of a system.

Canis Antiquus – the technologist that has not kept up their skills and should not be trusted with newer technologies.

Metrosexualus – these are the ethical hacking geeks who believe themselves and their work to be sexy but do not let their narcissism impact the quality of their work.

Egomaniacus Technum – the know-it-all that looks down upon everyone, especially other technical people. They make everyone feel like simpletons.

Ineptus Maximus – the guy that passed his CEH exam and believes he is now a hacking genius. He is not. This group represents those who's opinion should never be trusted.

Solus Maximus – the Ethical Hacker that likes to do everything alone. They are unable to work well in a team.

Novellus – the newbie Ethical Hacker that is still learning the business and has the potential to be good.

Mongus – the specialist who is great for tackling those special technologies.

Trancendo – the gifted Ethical Hacker that seems to know everything about the world of information security but does not flaunt their knowledge.

Like life and good tequila, the profiles need to be taken with a few grains of salt. They are characteristics that we as sage leaders need to be able to recognize in our people and then manage. By manage, I mean you may want to pair up that *Theoreticus Maximus* – or person who is more a researcher and theorist – with one of the more practical breeds that will compliment this individual and actually do the work, such as *Destroius Maximus* or *Transcendo*.

Finally, a word of warning. As tempting as it may be to share with your Ethical Hackers this new insight into their origins, it is imperative to remember that nearly all of these little rascals will loath being pigeonholed or classified by management (by themselves is another matter all together). Each one of your Ethical Hackers thinks of him or herself as a unique and special individual, and we certainly do not want to damage their fragile self-esteem, if it is indeed possible to damage it.

Should you dare approach an Ethical Hacker with your enlightened assessment of their character, you will likely find that their reaction will not be similar to your own (if you were to be pigeonholed in a similar manner) – that is, loud guffaws and spitting up of fine wine through the nose. In fact, reactions will likely vary from a few tears, to calls home to mommy, to a nose in the air as they walk out the door to a better gig.

Therefore, it is best to keep this guide tucked safely away

for amusement and reference; to be used to better understand the various personalities within the Ethical Hacker world and how to deal with their unique handling needs.

ABOUT THE AUTHOR

Over the past twenty years Mr Willburn has found himself face-down in the oily sands of Kuwait with the US Marines, floating down the mighty Juba River in Africa atop an Amtrak, and years later (after a particularly successful website launch), it found him passed out underneath the boardroom table with the founders of the dot-com where he got his start in information technology.

He has dined with real silverware and cloth napkins aboard high-flying airlines while jetting off to high-powered meetings in Europe as a Senior Manager at a Big-4 consulting agency; and has even dined with plastic forks and knifes while using his shirt as a napkin during his 'wilderness years' - aka the dot-bomb era. He has built and led teams of technology and security professionals in the commercial and Federal sectors, and currently leads ethical hacking gurus unto the breach as the head of the FBI's Enterprise Security Assessment Team; a group responsible for performing advanced security assessments on critical Bureau systems.

He has presented at the SANs Federal CIO briefings in Washington, D.C. and has been a member of several government working groups designed to improve security throughout the Federal Government, Department of Defense, and Intelligence Community.

He holds a B.Sc. from the London School of Economics and Political Science (which is where he gained some insight into the thinking of future world leaders aka the Wine'n Cheese Crowd) and has earned multiple security certifications...with various degrees of worth.